Absurd Alphabedtime Stories

**To Jennifer and Julia for
teaching me how to read.**

© 1976 by The Bethany Press

Library of Congress Cataloging in Publication Data
Hunter, Julius K.
    Absurd Alphabedtime Stories

    I. Nonsense-verses. (I. Alphabet books. 2. Animals—Poetry.
       3. Nonsense verses) I. Gomez, Ronald.

    II. Title.
    PZ8.3.H918Ab   811'.5'4   76-22534
ISBN 0-8272-0012-9

Manufactured in the U.S.A.

ABSURD ALPHABEDTIME STORIES

by

JULIUS K. HUNTER

art by

Ronald Gomez

You have here, friends, the A-B-C's,
With animals the features.
Give ear to letter sounds—and please—
Enjoy these silly creatures!

Appeasing an aardvark's appetite
Can keep you active day and night
Acquiring apples, apricots,
Ants, amoebas, anise dots,
Abalone, aphid tots,
Acorns, artichokes and lots
Of other foods that often make
An aardvark have a tummy ache.

Barracudas barely bite
The things they bump into at night.
But in the day they're very bright
And swim to chew things in their sight.

Crafty critters—crocodiles!
Take caution when a crocky smiles!
And when a crocky cries, my dears—
They certainly are not sincere tears!

Diving dolphins dripping drops
Of water on us all.
They're doubtless drenching us on porpoise,
And having quite a ball!

Emus eagerly embrace
When he-mus greet the she-mus.
And when they wed and find a place
The two-mus soon are three-mus.

Fearless foxes flash for fun
Their foxy grins for anyone!
They even smile when on the run
Outfoxing hounds. (Forgive the pun . . .)

Giant, gawking, great giraffe,
Why fear the gentle gerbil?
Just glimpse the rodent's photograph
And you will feel just terbil.

Hyenas ha-ha happily
As they run through the prairie
Ha-ha! Ha-ha! Ho-ho! Hee-hee!
How can they be so merry?

Ichneumons, incidentally,
Are cousins to mongooses.

Identical they are almost
But separate names each chooses.

Jerboa's jerky, jumping jaunts
In racing jamborees
Are helped along by jutting tails
And sprightly, springy knees!

Katydids keep kissing Katie.
What a kind and keen young lady!
Did Katie keep those kisses hidden?
Katie didden!

Lee lost Larry's little lynx
He lost it near the lawn he thynx.
Lee looks so hard he seldom blynx.
Let's hope he finds the missing lynx.

M

Mammoth, massive mastodon,
You should have your sneakers on.
You'd be much more a matchless menace
At major marathons of tennis.

Nancy needled nineteen nets
Of nylon for her newts.
Each newt is cute, but prone to scoot—
Nice, nervous little pets.

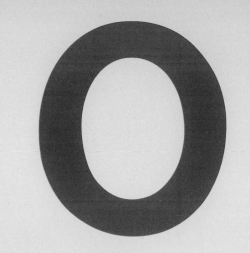

Octopusses occupy
Much more space than you or I.
The ocean's overly cramped and small
For all those arms to spread and sprawl.
I do not envy octopi!

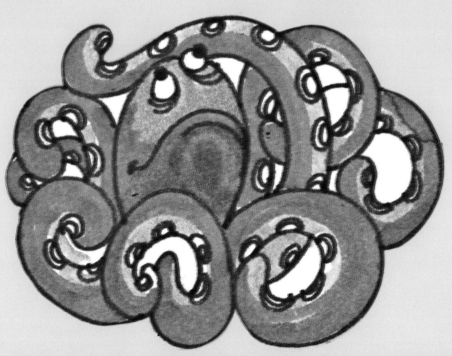

P

Porcupines pick prickly pears
And cactus plants to eat.
The porcu's food is cooked in pots
With low-flame prickly heat.

Quarrelsome quails quit quarreling quickly
And fly to the bushes to stand
'Cause birds in the bushes which cover them
    thickly
Are better than birds in the hand.

Q

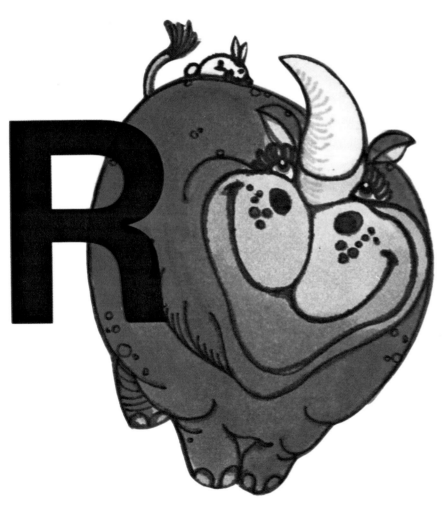

Rhinos rarely realize
Just how big they are in size—
And so they rip and run and play
And romp with rabbits every day.
Watch out! Be careful, playful bunny.
If a rhino falls on you it won't be funny!

Some say snakes seem sorta' sad,
But in the chats with snakes I've had
I've found them slithery—but glad
To slink and slide the way they do.
So some slow snakes don't show sharp smiles
They're merrier than crocodiles!

Two touring turtles took the train
To Texarkana in the rain.
The turtles took the tough terrain—
Next time they'll take an aeroplane.

Uniquely unusual Unicorns!
Upon their heads are uni-horns.
The unicorn's big boast, of course, is
You don't find horns on common horses.

Various vermin vex Venita.
She vents vague vows that they won't eat her.
Voicing votes they take her dare
And termites vow to eat her chair.

Walking with wild wallabies
Can tire your feet, your legs and knees.
For just when you would beg to stop
The wallaby still wants to hop.

X-ceedingly X-cellent X's X-ist
When two straight lines cross or two crooked
　　ones twist.
But no animal uses an X (what a shame!)
As the first lovely letter in spelling its name.

outhful yaks yawn, yelp and yap
efore they take their daily nap.
oo-hoo, you yaks! Sleep tight on your backs,
hen you can continue your yackity-yaks.

Zippy, zesty, zingy zebra
I wonder day and night

If your white stripes are painted on basic black
Or your black stripes are painted on white.

And there you have the A-B-C's—
And quite a funny zoo.
The animals have had a ball!
We hope that you have too!